Hampstead & Highgate

in old photographs, 1870-1918

1. Hampstead Heath on a Bank Holiday Monday in 1902, with Londoners — particularly East-Enders — enjoying themselves. On Bank Holidays, which were established in 1871, Hampstead could expect 200,000 to 300,000 visitors if the weather was fine.

2 *(overleaf)*. The fire station, Heath Street, in June 1903. It was built in 1873 on the site of the police station, which removed to the top of Rosslyn Hill when the Red Lion public house was demolished. The police station later moved to its present site at the corner of Downshire Hill.

LONDON AS IT WAS

ROFF & SON
BUILDERS & DECORATORS
UNDERTAKER
ELECTRICAL ENGINEERS
JUNE 22
HEATH STREET
FIRE

Hampstead & Highgate
in old photographs, 1870-1918

by

CHRISTINA M. GEE
Archivist, London Borough of Camden, 1965–1974

LONDON AS IT WAS

High Hill Press
in association with
Lionel Leventhal

First published 1974

by

High Hill Press
6–7 Hampstead High Street, London, N.W.3

in association with

Lionel Leventhal,
CBL Publishing Development Limited,
16 Pembridge Road, London W.11

SBN 0 904500 00 4

To Christopher Oxford

Printed in Great Britain by
Kingprint Limited,
Richmond, Surrey

Contents

3. The old beech tree under which Edward Irving preached in the grounds of Tudor House, Upper Terrace. The tree was blown down in the summer of 1911. Edward Irving (1792–1834), a minister of the Church of Scotland, founded the Catholic Apostolic Church. His followers built a church, now called Christ the King, in Gordon Square.

Acknowledgements

I would like to express my grateful thanks to the two major collections from which most of these photographs were drawn: the London Borough of Camden Local History Department and the Highgate Literary and Scientific Institution. Numbers 1–5, 7–10, 12–33, 35, 38–108 and 110–123 are from the Camden Local History Library in the Swiss Cottage Library; numbers 6 and 124–163 are from the Highgate Literary and Scientific Institution; number 11 is from the Imperial War Museum; numbers 34, 36 and 37 are from Christopher Oxford and number 109 is from Keats House, Hampstead. Most of these photographs were given to Camden Library and to Highgate by various people, and I would like to thank the following for their original generosity: London Transport Executive for numbers 2, 8 13–18, 21–25, 45, 47–48, 53–54, 57–59 and 61–80; Quaritch-Wrentmore Collection for number 5; the Sulman Collection for numbers 6, 124, 129, 131, 137, 141, 145, 146, 153 and 155; Miss Barrs for numbers 31 and 38; J. P. R. Lyell for numbers 51 and 106–107; the Garner Collection for numbers 85–90, 92 and 121; W. A. Cochrane for number 105; W. H. Ellis for numbers 126, 139, 142, 144 and 154; Mr. Watson for numbers 148, 149, 162 and 163; Fred Holland Day for number 109; L. Green for number 103; and Miss A. D. Phipps for number 101.

I would also like to thank William R. Maidment, Director of Libraries and Arts, London Borough of Camden; Mrs. G. Gosling, Librarian, Highgate Literary and Scientific Institution; Malcolm Holmes, Local History Librarian, Camden Public Library; I. G. Murray, Archivist, London Borough of Haringey; Miss M. van Reenen and Christopher Oxford for their hard work and encouragement.

FURTHER READING

BAINES, F. E. ed. *Records of the manor, parish and borough of Hampstead . . . to December 31st 1889,* 1890.

BARRATT, Thomas J. *The Annals of Hampstead,* 3v., 1912; reprint, Lionel Leventhal, 1972.

HOWITT, William. *The northern heights of London*, 1869.

JEALOUS, Walter K. *Highgate Village,* 1919.

LLOYD, John H. *History, topography and antiquities of Highgate in the county of Middlesex . . .*, 1888.

LYSONS, Daniel. *The Environs of London,* 1796; 2nd ed., 1811.

MAXWELL, Anna. *Hampstead.* [1912].

NORRIE, Ian, ed. *The Heathside Book of Hampstead and Highgate,* 1962.

NORRIE, Mavis and Ian, eds. *The Book of Hampstead,* rev. ed., 1968.

PARK, John James. *The Topography and Natural History of Hampstead in the County of Middlesex,* rev. ed., 1818.

PRICKETT, Frederick. *The History and Antiquities of Highgate, Middlesex,* 1842; reprint, 1971.

SURVEY OF LONDON. Vol. 17: *The Village of Highgate,* 1936.

THOMPSON, F. M. L. *Hampstead: Building a Borough, 1650–1964,* 1974.

THORNE, James. *Handbook to the Environs of London,* 2v., 1876.

WADE, Christopher, ed. *Streets of Hampstead,* 1972.

WADE, Christopher, ed. *More Streets of Hampstead,* 1973.

Introduction

Hampstead and Highgate are areas rich in local history. By comparison, districts like Camden Town and Clapham hardly give a sense of history except, perhaps, where one sees the odd old building. But in Hampstead and Highgate the past is always present. Old houses abound and the original street patterns remain to remind one of the Hampstead Town and Highgate Village that residents have always been proud to give as their address.

Local history, however, is not only the study of notable persons and buildings but also of the local people who never made the headlines but who nevertheless contributed to the history of their town or village. Hampstead and Highgate may have been the home and haunt of poets like Keats and Coleridge and of artists such as Constable and Romney, but they were also the home and haunt of ordinary people — some of whom were captured by the camera and continue to show what it was really like to live in these areas some seventy years ago.

During the period covered by the photographs in this book — 1870 to 1918 — great changes were made, particularly on the edges of the borough in Kilburn and West Hampstead and also around the Archway. The high streets were crowded with small shops serving the local population and here were to be found the cobbler, the baker, the draper, the bookseller and the music-seller. Hampstead is lucky in that it still has four businesses that have survived the passage and ravages of time: Forster's, the grocers; King's, the stationers; Knowles-Brown, the jewellers; and Stamp's, the chemists.

In his book *The Environs of London,* 1876, James Thorne

4 *(overleaf).* The opening of University College School, Frognal, by His Majesty King Edward VII, 26th July 1907.

describes Hampstead as follows:

> The *Town* straggles up the slopes of the hill, towards the Heath on the top, in an odd, sideling, tortuous, irregular, and unconnected fashion. There are the fairly broad winding High Street, and other good streets and lanes, lined with large old brick houses within high-walled enclosures, over which lean ancient trees, and alongside them houses small and large, without a scrap of garden, and only a very little dingy yard; narrow and dirty byways, courts, and passages, with steep flights of steps, and mean and crowded tenements; fragments of open green spaces, and again streets and lanes bordered with shady elms and limes. On the whole, however, the pleasanter and sylvan character prevails, especially W. of the main street. The trees along the streets and lanes are the most characteristic and redeeming feature of the village.

To combat the problem of the 'mean and crowded tenements' the Hampstead Town Improvements were proposed. The Hampstead Vestry had been trying for a number of years to clear some of the slum alleys and courts at the top of the High Street, and an opportunity came with the building of Fitzjohn's Avenue in 1871. Between 1876 and 1882 various proposals and plans were discussed: the tradespeople, who feared loss of trade, wanted the new Fitzjohn's Avenue to turn into Perrin's Lane and so into the High Street; but the gentry preferred to extend Heath Street by demolishing Little Church Row and various alleys and courts and so speed their way to the Heath. Eventually, a plan was approved and the Metropolitan Street Improvement Act was passed in 1883. This allowed the demolition of Baker's Row (a 'bridged' alley similar to Perrin's Court), Crockett's Court, Johnson's Yard, Oriel Court and the Yorkshire Grey Yard. Three public houses were lost in the demolition: the Black Boy and Still, the Cock and Crown and the Yorkshire Grey. But the Three Horseshoes was rebuilt. The work was completed and the new road, lower Heath Street, was opened in May 1887. The cost of the improvements was £137,813 — half of which was paid by the ratepayers of Hampstead.

Hampstead High Street was again disrupted between 1903 and 1907 when the route of what was to become the Northern Line of the Underground was being prepared. Indeed, several of the photographs in this book were taken by E. Milner, staff photographer to the Northern Railway Company, as an official precaution against fraudulent

5. A knifeboard bus seen at the junction of Rosslyn Hill with Downshire Hill in June 1887. The house with the sixteen chimneys is still standing. The bus, which ran between Hampstead and Piccadilly, had to have an extra horse to pull it up the High Street. These horses became so familiar with the routine that when they were unhitched at the top of the High Street they made their own way down to the bottom of Rosslyn Hill and waited for the next bus. The journey from Hampstead to Piccadilly took about an hour.

claims for compensation by residents in the houses above the route of the line. When cracks or subsidence were claimed to be the result of the tunnelling, proof of existing cracks and the like could be shown and compensation would be paid only for damage genuinely caused by the Underground. These photographs cover the whole of the route of the Northern Line from where it enters the London Borough of Camden at Tottenham Court Road to where it leaves it beyond Jack Straw's Castle. They were presented to the Hampstead and St. Pancras Libraries by the London Transport Executive in 1961.

Kilburn and West Hampstead were the fastest growing parts of Hampstead during the later half of the nineteenth century. The population doubled in the 1880s and increased by half as much again in the 1890s. In 1901, Kilburn Ward had 79 persons to the acre — nearly three times as many per acre as elsewhere in the Borough . . . although the controlling upper middle classes, who were clustered around the top of the hill, were outnumbered two to one by their servants. Highgate's population was also increasing at this time, as Thorne remarks when he describes that area's lack of open space and building land:

> On the W. . . . are the Grove and Green, where was the large pond . . ., now filled up and planted. The Green, bordered by groves of ancient elms, seems to have been the centre of the original village, and the place where the villagers

met for rural games and holiday diversions. . . . Lanes run off rt. and l., from the Grammar School to Hornsey, from the Gatehouse to Hampstead, main road and lanes being alike lined with good old tree-embowered houses, modern villas with bright gardens, and comfortable cottages; not without signs of dirt or poverty, but, as a whole, a healthy, prosperous and pleasant place . . . but vacant spaces whence the view [of London] was obtainable have been so enclosed or built over that it is now hard to find a tolerable stand-point, unless it be on a house-top.'

The coming of the tramway in 1884 made a terrific difference to Highgate, for it negotiated the steep gradient of Highgate Hill with ease where once it had taken heavy wagons the best part of the day.

Looking through the photographs for this book and making the final selection gave me a great deal of pleasure. It has always been a mystery to me why authors looking for illustrative material for a local history prefer a badly executed watercolour or engraving to a good photograph. Photographs seem to me to be much more immediate, and they often contain fascinating cameos of the man-in-the-street and his surroundings as they really were rather than as portrayed by a painter with artist's licence. Peruse these photographs — and see if you don't agree.

6. The Archway. This rare photograph shows the pedestrian tunnel under the Archway provided in c.1880. It was made by tunnelling through the hillside on the west side of the Archway.

Hampstead

7. The Hampstead horse-bus on the west side of Rosslyn Hill.

J. H. KILLICK & Co Photographers
SEP 16 1908

8 *(opposite).* Number 38 Haverstock Hill in September 1903. It is still standing.

9. Rosslyn Hill, looking south, c.1900. Note the Beverly Coffee Shop on the corner of Willoughby Road, now removed to Finchley Road.

10 *(below).* The Shepherd's Cottage in the grounds of Rosslyn House, 1880. The house was demolished in 1896.

11. Rookies of the Royal Flying Corps in the First World War, 'somewhere in Hampstead'. They were just leaving what appears to be the quartermaster's stores with their initial kit issue.

12. The Rosslyn Hill Auxiliary Hospital in Rosslyn Lodge. The hospital was operational from October 1916 to December 1919.

13, 14 *(opposite).* Numbers 4, 5 and 6 Hampstead High Street in 1903. Although mostly demolished now, the upper part of Number 6 remains. The site is now occupied by the High Hill Bookshop.

15, 16 *(overleaf).* Numbers 11 and 12 Hampstead High Street in September 1903. The High Hill Bookshop continued the tradition of a bookshop on this site formerly occupied by Hewetson, later by Mason and then by Alfred Wilson, who went into liquidation in 1956. In 1957 the company was reconstructed as the High Hill Bookshop and later moved to 6–6a Hampstead High Street. Notice that very few books had attractive dust-jackets in those days. The shop has since been rebuilt and is now the Midland Bank. Old Bank House is still standing.

F. POOLE
PHOLSTERER
AT 43 HEATH ST
RIDE
GARDNER CYCLES
FITTED WITH
£200 REWARD
SEP 17 1908

SEP 17 1908

TSON,
NER &
OKSELLER.
BASS
BASS
& Co's
PALE
ALE
SEP 17 1908
DEWAR'S
WHISKY

17. The King of Bohemia, September 1903. It has since been rebuilt. The name commemorates the marriage of Elizabeth, daughter of James I, to Frederick V, the Elector Palatine of Bohemia.

18. Numbers 13 and 14 Hampstead High Street in 1903. Both buildings are still there, but Old Bank House — originally number 13 — is now number 14 and the shop that was Fleming Reid & Co. is now number 15 Hampstead High Street.

LEMING REID & Co
NERS & MANUFACTURERS
E WORSTED MILLS
REENOCK
SCOTCH WOO
& HOSIERY
STORES
150 BRANCHES
SEP 17 1908
SCOTCH WOOL & HOSIERY STORE

19. Hampstead High Street. This photograph was taken before 1870, when Gayton Road was built. Gayton Road now occupies the sites of the shops of D. A. Simon & Co., Tanner's and the shop next door, which was rebuilt as half a house and became the tobacconist's that used to be at the corner of Gayton Road.

TANNER
D.A.SIMON & Co

20. The electrification of Hampstead, 1905. Workmen laying the mains at Gayton Crescent pose for a photograph. The workmen's tent carries the words 'Hampstead Vestry Electricity Department' despite the fact that the Vestry had become the Borough Council five years earlier.

21 *(opposite).* The entrance to Flask Walk in June 1903. The bridge rooms fell down in 1911 and were not replaced.

22, 23 *(overleaf).* Numbers 43 and 44 Hampstead High Street in June 1903. They have since been rebuilt. King's, the stationers — one of the oldest businesses in the High Street — have moved across the road to the other side of the High Street.

RIDING MASTER
SADDLE
HORSES ON HIRE
for any Period.
RIDING & DRIVING TAUGHT.
F. DAVEY
HORSES TAKEN IN TO LIVERY
PRIVATE RESIDENCE, 64, HIGH STREET
SMITH'S PATENT
HOVIS BREAD
CURES INDIGESTION
MAZAWATTEE COCOA
JUNE 17 08
20
14
12

W & H. KING
KINGS STATIONERY & ARTISTS STORES
FORMERLY
THE OLD POST OFFICE
JUNE 17
FRYS
CHOCOLATE

RIDING
& DRIVI
TAI
SMITH'S
PATENT
HOV
TORES
HOVIS BREAD
PROMOTES DIGESTION
AS SUPPLIED TO HIS MAJESTY THE KING
FRYS
CHOCOLATE
PEEK FREAN
BISCUITS
LONDON
JUNE 17 08
ROBBS
BISCUITS

24, 25. Numbers 47–48 and 49–50 Hampstead High Street in 1903. All the buildings were demolished.

Hampstead Underground Station stands on the site of 49–50.

26. Flask Walk, seen here in 1910, takes its name from the flasks of spa water sold at the Lower Flask Tavern. The cottages were built for the local workmen.

27. Shops in Hampstead High Street, c. 1908, including one of the oldest — Forster's, which was established in 1790 — and showing the entrance to Perrin's Court. The trees mark the present site of the offices of the Hampstead and Highgate Express.

28. Perrin's Lane, off Hampstead High Street, in 1910. The William IV Tavern was originally called the King's Head, but the name was changed in 1835 when William IV paid a visit to Hampstead. The weatherboard building is no longer to be seen but the lamp post is still there.

29 *(opposite).* The parish church of St. John, Hampstead, in Church Row, 1912. The additions to the church were dedicated in June 1912 by the Rt. Rev. the Bishop of London, who announced at the same time that the Deanery of Hampstead was to be made an Archdeaconry.

30 *(top).* Church Row, c.1907. Note the beginning of the present parking problem . . .

31. Church Row, c. 1910. The cart is one of the Hampstead Borough Council's dust-carts.

32. Old houses in Church Row, demolished in May 1898; now the site of Gardnor Mansions.

33. Frognal, c.1907. No one seems able to account for the origins of the name Frognal, which is one of the oldest placenames in the Hampstead area. The building on the left is Priory Lodge — named after Frognal Priory, which was close by.

34 *(top)*. Hampstead High Street, looking south, prior to the Town Improvements in 1886. The Bird in Hand public house, on the left, was built in 1878 and was the terminus for the horse-bus. Most of the shops on the right were demolished and later rebuilt.

35. The top of Hampstead High Street, showing the Black Boy and Still — one of the public houses that was pulled down in 1886 as part of the Town Improvements. The Cock and Crown and the Yorkshire Grey were also lost.

36 *(top)*. Little Church Row, c.1885, showing the Three Horseshoes public house and adjacent shops holding closing-down sales prior to rebuilding during the Town Improvements. The entrance in the centre of the photograph is one of the many insanitary alleys and courts that connected Little Church Row with Hampstead High Street.

37. Little Church Row, 1885. These buildings were demolished so that the lower end of Heath Street could join the newly completed Fitzjohn's Avenue and so provide a main thoroughfare from Hampstead to London. Notice, in the centre, that a 'Genuine Sale' is being held and that 'To effect an Immediate Sale a Great Sacrifice will be made'. These were clearly the 'Last Few Days'.

38. The top of Fitzjohn's Avenue, showing the entrance to Little Church Row — now Heath Street — in 1886.

39. Bradley's Buildings in 1886. This was an alley at the north end of Little Church Row, the northern end of which became Holly Bush Vale after the southern end was demolished during the Town Improvements in 1887. The children were most probably from Hampstead parochial schools. Note the tilt in the top of the fire station tower.

40. Little Church Row in 1886, just before demolition. Note the narrowness of the road. The cart is being loaded with pews from the Primitive Methodist Church. A chimneysweep occupied Oriel House at this time.

41. The Yorkshire Grey Tavern in Yorkshire Grey Yard, named after it, in 1880. The yard was a cul-de-sac entered from Little Church Row.

42. Yorkshire Grey Yard, looking from the tavern. This and other criss-cross alleys were demolished in 1886 to link Heath Street with Fitzjohn's Avenue as part of the Town Improvements.

43. Holly Bush Hill in 1886, showing the back of the fire station and the twist in the roof of the tower — which had to be removed later. The demolition works in progress at the top of the High Street were part of the Town Improvements.

44. Holly Bush Hill, c.1910.

45 *(opposite)*. Heath Street, looking towards the High Street, June 1903. Very little of the original buildings remains.

THE TYNEMAINCOAL Co LTD
ORDER OFFICE.
GEORG
MESSENGER & Co
JUNE 17 06
PRICES
TYNE MAIN PER TON
BEST
SECONDS
CUBES
KITCHEN
NUTS
COBBLES
STOVE
LOWEST SUMMER PRICES
BEST HOUSE COALS ONLY
COALS.
HAMPSTEAD

46 *(facing).* Golden Yard, off Heath Street, showing artisans' dwellings in 1909. The name Golden is a corruption of Goulding's Yard. The Goulding family occupied and owned the property c.1574–1779.

47 *(top).* The Mount Square, formerly Golden Square, May 1904 — described by Daphne du Maurier in one of her books as 'a little square of slum houses'.

48. Old cottages in The Grove, May 1904. These were built as working class dwellings. Until 1926, Number 12 was occupied by Mary Webb, authoress of *Precious Bane,* part of which was said to have been written there.

49. The White Bear, New End, c.1910 — one of the oldest public houses in Hampstead. The stone set in the wall above the bow-window reads 'MS 1704'. The inn has since been rebuilt. During the last century sports events were held in front of the White Bear, including the greasy pole and running races.

50. Willow Buildings, New End Square. This incredibly foreshortened photograph gives the impression that Burgh House, in the centre of the picture, was part of the Militia Barracks. But this was not so. Note Weatherall Place, in the foreground, where the horse and coachman can be seen. The barracks were built in 1863 and partially demolished by 1915, when Weatherall Place was widened into Well Walk.

51. Hampstead Wells, Well Walk, c.1907. The chalybeate springs of Hampstead were famous in Charles II's time; and from about 1700, throughout the eighteenth century, Hampstead was a spa — though not as fashionable as Bath or Tunbridge Wells. Water from the wells could be had every day from various places in London including the Greyhound in King Street, Bloomsbury.

52. The original 'lock-up' at Cannon Hall, 1910. Cannon Hall was often the residence of magistrates, and the 'lock-up' in the wall was connected to the garden of Cannon Hall by a passage. The 'lock-up' was known to have been there in 1730, and it was still in use in 1832.

53. Number 61 Haverstock Hill, 1903.

54. The George, Haverstock Hill, July 1903. The George is one of a group of buildings originally known as Bellevue. At one time, there were tea gardens in front of the tavern.

55. Hampstead Town Hall, c.1890. It was built in 1877–8. Prior to that, the meetings of the Vestry had been held in the Workhouse (now Hospital) in New End. Sergeant Rowbottom and his wife, of the Militia Barracks in Willow Road, were appointed the first caretakers at thirty shillings a week.

56. The complimentary dinner of the Vestry of St. John, Hampstead, given to Sir Henry Harben, Chairman of the Vestry, in the Throne Room of the Holborn Restaurant, 28th October 1897. Sir Henry was the first Mayor of the new Hampstead Borough Council in 1900. Harben Parade, Finchley Road, is named after him.

192
JULY 7 08

57 *(opposite)*, 58 *(above left)* and 59 *(above right)*. Numbers 192, 194 and 196 Haverstock Hill in 1903. These buildings were demolished and the site is now 210–228 Haverstock Hill.

60 *(overleaf)*. England's Lane. This photograph was taken some time between 1897 and 1906. The shops were built on land that had previously been occupied by the Hampstead Cricket Club. The lane is shown on Rocque's map of 1745 and takes its name from James England, to whom Chalcotes Farm was leased in 1776.

RAWORTH
HOUSEHOLD & TOILET
SOAPS
HOUSEHOLD & TOILET
SOAPS
FRESH OR SALT
LONDON & SUBURBAN
EXPRESS CARRIERS

DEC 3 1908

62 *(above left)*. Number 141 Haverstock Hill, 1903.

63 *(above right)*. Number 145 Haverstock Hill, 1903.

61 *(opposite)*. Number 149 Havestock Hill, 1903.

64 *(above left).* Number 137 Haverstock Hill, 1903.

65 *(above right).* Number 99 Haverstock Hill, 1903.

66 *(above left).* Number 139 Haverstock Hill, 1903.

67 *(above right).* Number 117 Haverstock Hill, 1903.

COMBE & Co's
Celebrated OLD & MILD ALES
E. H. Blunt
SPECIAL WHIS
KILMARNOCK
CHOPS & STEAKS
TEA & COFFEE
FEB 16 08
BASS & Co's PALE ALE
HOT LUNCHEONS FROM 1 TO 2.30
COMBE & Co's CELEBRATED ALES
COMBE & Co's STOUT
BILLIARDS
POOL

69. The Load of Hay Tavern in March 1903. It was originally called the Cart and Horses, and for a number of years it was known as The Noble Art due to the gymnasium of the British Boxing Board of Control situated behind the pub. The name The Load of Hay was reinstated in 1974. This tavern is one of many conveniently spaced on the roads leading out of London and it was originally frequented by waggoners.

68 *(opposite)*. The Sir Richard Steele in February 1903. Sir Richard Steele (1672–1729), after whom this pub was named, was co-author with Joseph Addison of the *Spectator*. They invented the character Sir Roger de Coverley. Steele had a cottage on Haverstock Hill. It was demolished in 1867.

70. Number 73 Haverstock Hill, 1903. This terrace of shops is still standing.

71 *(opposite, left)*. Number 75 Haverstock Hill, 1903.

72 *(opposite, right)*. Number 77 Haverstock Hill, 1903.

73 *(opposite, below left)*. Number 79 Haverstock Hill, 1903.

74 *(opposite, below right)*. Number 81 Haverstock Hill, 1903.

73
75 K. HAGEDORN TAILOR 75
DYERS
FEB 13 08
MADAME ALINE
PARISIAN DRESSMAKER

EDORN TAILOR 75
DYERS AND MARKS & Co. CLEANERS
79
FEB 13 08
PARISIAN DRESSMAKER
THE CLEANING DYEING & BLEACHING

LEANERS.
79 · F.M. HOLDSWORTH · 79
81 W.
FEB 13 08
BOVRIL

LDSWORTH · 79
81 W. PARNELL.
FEB 13 08
BOVRIL

ALBt WEST.
London House.
50
50
BRICKS.
SAND.
BALLAST.
Grey LIME.
Chalk Do
Lias Do
WHITING
PLASTER
And
CEMENTS
ALBt WEST
BUILDERS'
MERCHANT
LADDERS
SCAFFOLDING
SLATES
TILES
GOODS
FEB 12 08

76 *(above left).* Numbers 56 and 56a Haverstock Hill, 1903.

77 *(above right).* Number 58 Haverstock Hill, 1903.

75 *(facing).* Number 50 Haverstock Hill, 1903.

78. Number 70 Haverstock Hill, 1903.

79. Number 20 Haverstock Hill, 1903.

80. The Adelaide public house, Chalk Farm, in February 1903. The pyramids game advertised in the upper windows was a form of snooker. It was also played at Ye Olde Bull and Bush. The 'ghost' figure is a result of movement during the long exposure necessary to take the photograph.

Swiss Cottage and Finchley Road

81. The toll-gate at the Swiss Cottage Tavern. The tavern was one of the first buildings here, and from 1840 until the removal of the toll-gate in July 1871 travellers could refresh themselves before paying their tolls and using the new road to Finchley.

82. The Swiss Cottage Tavern, c.1870. Running races were held here. The short-distance races were run from the Swiss Cottage to the site of the new Public Baths in the Finchley New Road (now Sainsbury's).

83. Fitzjohn's Avenue when it was still a track leading from the bottom of Belsize Lane to Hampstead. This picture was taken from a house half way up Belsize Lane. Fitzjohn's Avenue was built up from 1871 onwards and was an immediate success. It was considered to be one of the most beautiful avenues in London. Notice the two boys — one in his 'Lord Fauntleroy' suit.

84. College Crescent, at the turn of the century. The crescent takes its name from the theological college for non-conformists that was built on what is now the site of Northways. The college was built in 1851 and pulled down in 1934. The imposing bank building at the corner was standing until quite recently.

85. Holy Trinity Church, Finchley Road, prior to the First World War. The church was built in 1872 on land given by the Lord of the Manor, Sir John Maryon Wilson. It is to be demolished in 1974 and rebuilt on a smaller scale.

86. Finchley Road, showing John Barnes' old building, the cab rank, Finchley Road station and Holy Trinity Church.

87. Finchley Road, looking north from the corner of Frognal. The postcard is dated 20th December 1902.

88. One of a series of post-card views of Swiss Cottage and the surrounding roads. College Crescent, c.1892, showing the newly built Fitzjohn's Avenue. The original pink chestnut trees that lined Fitzjohn's Avenue were later replaced with plane trees.

89. Swiss Cottage, looking north and showing Finchley Road, the Non-Conformist College, College Crescent, Eton Avenue and the Blind School.

90. Finchley Road, looking north and showing the New College — now the site of Northways flats and shops — and College Crescent.

88.

89.

90.

91.

Finchley Rd, N.W.

92.

DAIRY
THE FARMS
THE NURSERY MILK
THREE POINTS GUARANTEED
PURITY-QUALITY-CLEANLINESS
SWISS COTTAGE DAIRY
PEARS
The Swiss Cottage, Finchley Road

93.

SWISS COTTAGE STATION
S. MILLS
FORBES
Swiss Cottage and Belsize Road

91. Finchley Road, looking south towards St. John's Wood. Almost all the buildings on either side of the road have been replaced.

92. The dairy, the stables, the Swiss Cottage Tavern, the bus terminus and the view south down Finchley Road.

93. Upper Avenue Road, the dairy, Finchley Road, Swiss Cottage station and Belsize Road. The poster advertising Fuchs dates the post-card to 1892, when the cellist appeared in London.

21 M. WHELLEN
NOTICES
M. WHELLENS.

95. A road accident at the corner of Heath Drive and Finchley Road. This picture was taken between 9 o'clock and 10 o'clock on the morning of 17th April 1916.

96. A family outing bicycling in the Finchley Road, c.1907. This would be a rather dangerous pastime today.

94 *(opposite)*. The Hampstead Public Baths in the Finchley New Road, on ground formerly occupied by the skating rink. The baths were opened on 5th June 1888, when this picture was taken. Sainsbury's supermarket now occupies the site.

97 *(top)*. The Lymington Road Depot. This photograph, taken after the formation of the Hampstead Borough Council in 1900, shows the Council's dust-carts lined up for inspection.

98 *(middle)*. Hampstead Borough Council workmen, with their water-carts and horses, posing for a photograph at the Lymington Road Depot.

99. A charabanc outing for the staff of the Lithos Road Electricity Station. The station was built in 1894 by the Hampstead Vestry and it supplied power to Hampstead until nationalisation in 1948.

Kilburn and West Hampstead

100. Kilburn High Road, c.1905. The bank on the right is at the junction with Belsize Road. Compare this picture with the next one.

101. Kilburn High Road, at the junction with Eresby Road, c.1870. During the last thirty years of the last century Kilburn and West Hampstead were the fastest growing areas.

102. West End Lane, showing the Old Black Lion before it was rebuilt in 1911–12.

103. West End Green, c.1890. Kilburn and West Hampstead changed rapidly from rural hamlets with the opening up of the St. John's Wood (Metropolitan) Railway. West End Lane was so lonely and quiet in 1870 that people were afraid to walk along it.

104. The Old Cock and Hoop, West End Green, which had very fine tea-gardens. It was closed in 1896 and was eventually pulled down in 1902 to make way for Alexandra Mansions.

105. A gypsy encampment on Fortune Green, West Hampstead, 1887.

106 *(top).* Emmanuel School, West Hampstead, in 1907. The building is still standing and in use as a school.

107. A maypole dance in Emmanuel Church Vicarage garden, West Hampstead, in 1907.

South End Green

108 *(top)*. Downshire Hill postal sorting office. Within the parish of Hampstead in 1891 there were twenty-seven post offices and two sorting offices — this one and one in Kilburn. The total force of postmen was over a hundred. The building still stands and is now used by the Department of Health and Social Security.

109. Keats House (Wentworth Place), Keats Grove. In 1890, when this photograph was taken, the house was called Lawn Bank and was in John Street. The name of the street was changed in 1909 and that of the house in 1920, when it was purchased by the Keats Memorial Committee. Note the absence of the ivy 'armchair' around the front door.

110. South End Road, c.1900, looking towards Hampstead Heath. The row of shops still stands — including Rumbold's, which was then also the post office and seemed to have a Royal Warrant. Heathhurst Road was built from 1894–1900. The cab rank has now disappeared.

111. A 1900 poster of the North London Railway — an independent company. This copy was found by a signalman at Broad Street ticket office during demolitions there in June 1957. Hampstead Heath Station was opened in 1860. On Easter Monday, 18th April 1892, eight people lost their lives in a serious crush on the stairs. The locomotive is a 4-4-OT originally designed by William Adams for the NLR in 1868. The class eventually contained 78 engines, the last of which was taken out of service in 1929.

Hampstead Heath

112. Bank Holiday Monday, Hampstead Heath, 1902.

113. **The Whitestone Pond**, looking towards Bellmoor — the home of Thomas J. Barratt, author of *The Annals of Hampstead*. It was called the Whitestone Pond because of its proximity to the white milestone indicating four miles from St. Giles' Pound. Originally a horse pond, it was always the first of the Hampstead ponds to freeze in winter and provide skating.

114. The Whitestone Pond, looking towards Golders Green, c.1890. The pond was enlarged by the Vestry in 1875. George du Maurier, the *Punch* illustrator, was inspired by the donkeys galloping around the pond to conceive his 'Ponds Asinorum'.

115. Jack Straw's Castle, 1905. The inn, which was first mentioned in the Court Rolls in 1713, takes its name from Jack Straw, a leader of the Peasant's Revolt in 1381. It is said that his followers assembled here prior to joining him at Highbury.

116. Ye Olde Bull and Bush, c.1907. Made famous by Hogarth — and later made legendary by Florrie Forde — the building was extensively rebuilt in 1924. The car park replaces the gardens where Constable, Romney, Gainsborough and Sir Joshua Reynolds enjoyed themselves.

117 *(right)*. The garden of Ye Olde Bull and Bush, 1880. The low tree in the background was there in Hogarth's time. The pub was at one time the country house of William Hogarth, who is said to have laid out the gardens.

118. **The Vale of Health, Hampstead Heath.** This photograph was taken from an aeroplane and is postmarked 23rd May 1907. The large building on the right, formerly the Athenaeum, was the home of the Salvation Army from 1882 to 1886.

119. Hampstead, from Parliament Hill, 1905. There were sheep on the Heath during the Second World War and right up to May 1952.

120. Hampstead Heath, c.1890. Known as 'London's lung', the Heath was rescued in 1871 from the development plans of the late Lord of the Manor, Sir Thomas Maryon Wilson (d.1869). John Gurney Hoare and the Copyholders of Hampstead had opposed the building plans of Sir Thomas for forty years. The Metropolitan Board of Works, later the L.C.C. then purchased the Heath from his brother for £47,000. Since then, additions have been continually made to it — including Parliament Hill Fields (1885) and Kenwood (1924).

121. Wyldes's Farm, formerly Collin's Farm and also Tooley's Farm. In 1823 it was the residence of John Linnell, the painter. The farm lands were bought by the L.C.C. and added to Hampstead Heath in 1907.

122. The Spaniard's Inn, looking east, c.1911. The inn stands on the site of a lodge occupied at one time by the keeper of the toll-gate, on the right. This gate formed one of the entrances to the Bishop of London's park.

123. The Spaniard's Inn, looking west, c.1905. At the time of the Gordon Riots, in 1780, Kenwood was saved from destruction by the landlord of the Spaniard's, who offered the rioters drink while he sent word to Lord Chief Justice Mansfield, who ordered out the military and dispersed the rioters.

Highgate

124 *(above).* Lauderdale House, c.1890, showing the laying out of the flowerbeds by two of the gardeners.

125 *(opposite, above).* Highgate West Hill, c.1886, showing the milestone below the entrance to Baroness Burdett-Coutts' estate — now Robin Grove.

126 *(opposite, below).* A view of Highgate West Hill from the spire of St. Michael's Church in 1903 — when the spire was being repaired — showing Cutbush's Nursery; Holly Terrace; and Holly Lodge, the home of Baroness Burdett-Coutts.

127 *(above).* The Fox and Crown Inn, Highgate West Hill, c.1886. This inn, now demolished, was famous for the assistance given by the landlord to Queen Victoria when the wheel came off her carriage on Highgate West Hill in 1837. The Queen was made comfortable in the chair shown in the photograph while repairs were effected. Thereafter, the landlord was graciously permitted to show the Royal Coat of Arms — which is now in the library of the Highgate Literary and Scientific Institution. The inn was demolished in 1896, when Witanhurst was built.

128. The Flask public house, 1886. One of the oldest inns in Highgate, it is mentioned in the Court Roll of 1716. The water-cart in the foreground brought water to the cottages from the well in Southwood Lane. The two black spots in the road — centre left — are the landlord's hens, which then ran free in the quiet road.

129. Highgate High Street, looking south from the Angel Inn, c.1885.

BARC
FIRE
BRIGADE
STATION

130. The interior of the library of the Highgate Literary and Scientific Institution in South Grove, 1895. Mr. and Mrs. Holt were the librarians until 1904.

131 *(below)*. South Grove, 1890, opposite the Gatehouse, showing the police station and the Highgate Dispensary. It is now known as Highgate West Hill.

132 *(opposite, above)*. The top of Highgate High Street as it was in 1882, showing the old forge. This was known as Dodd's Corner — after the name of the blacksmith, who is standing in front of his forge.

133 *(opposite, below)*. This picture, probably taken from the roof of Number 21 Highgate High Street, shows the backs of the houses in South Grove. The house on the left, which is still there, is approached under an archway from the High Street. At the time of this photograph, and for many years later, it was let in rooms as a working-class tenement.

134. Highgate High Street in June 1899. The placards are advertising a Boer outrage and Captain Coe's final. The first was war news; the second, tips for the races. The building with the flagstaff was the Office of the Local Board (Hornsey).

135. The Gatehouse Tavern in 1886. On the right, the old toll-gate. The posts in front of the churchyard were to control the traffic passing through the toll-gate. The inn was rebuilt in the early 1930s.

JUDGE SENR
BASS
PALE ALE
2

5
2153

136 *(opposite, above).* The opening of the cable tramway in 1884 — the first in Europe. Steep gradients were tackled by underground cables worked by steam. The engine house from which the cable drum was operated stood just behind the shops in the High Street near Townsend's Yard.

137 *(opposite, below).* At the top of Highgate High Street. This photograph was probably taken during the early days of the tramway. It shows a Highgate schoolboy and the school chapel in the background.

138 *(above).* The Angel Inn in 1882. The original rather plain building was 'antiqued' some time between 1874 and 1882. The fire station mentioned on the lamp post was in North Road.

139 *(below).* The Bank, Highgate Hill, c.1900. The coal is being delivered to Channing House, which is now the site of School House. Some of the buildings below were destroyed in the Second World War.

140. The corner of Townsend's Yard and Highgate High Street, 1880. The shopkeeper standing in the doorway was Robert Rogers, the draper.

141. Highgate High Street, looking north, c.1880. Rogers', the drapers, is on the right.

142. Numbers 18 to 24 Highgate High Street, c.1880.

ALLSOPP'S
PALE & BURTON ALES

143 *(opposite, above).* Cottages in Townsend's Yard in 1885. Mr. Kerry, the builder, is holding a pole perpendicularly to show the state of these seventeenth-century cottages. The Brothers West, behind Mr. Kerry, were the village sweeps.

144 *(opposite, below).* Highgate Hill, c.1885, opposite St. Joseph's, showing the Old Crown Inn and Crown cottages. This picture was taken after the laying of the cable tramway since its chimney can be seen at the top of the hill. The children are watching the cable.

145 *(above).* Highgate Hill, 1880, showing Fairseat House — the home of Sir Sidney Waterlow, who presented the house and grounds to the London County Council in 1889. The grounds, which also included the gardens of Lauderdale House and Hertford House, are now Waterlow Park.

146 *(below).* Waterlow Park, c.1890, showing the gardens above the lake as laid out by the London County Council.

147. Southwood Lane in 1889, showing the Office of the Local (Hornsey) Board. Hornsey did not become a borough until 1903. In 1936 the building was sold to Lord Southwood, who had it pulled down.

148 *(top)*. The fire station was in North Road, next to St. Michael's School. This photograph shows two of the firemen and their equipment, c.1900.

149. Southwood Lane, 1906, showing the district sorting office and the post office staff.

150. The Red Lion and Sun public house in 1887. The landlord, Mr. Silvester, and his dogs are standing in the doorway.

151. Park House Passage, The Park, North Hill, 1886. The children are sitting in front of the pound, opposite Broadlands Road. Straying cattle were rounded up and put into the pound, the owner having to pay a fine to the Lord of the Manor to retrieve them.

152. Southwood Lane, 1886, showing the old village well. The wall on the left — demolished in 1960 — was the garden wall of Southwood House, built by General George Wade (1673–1748). The site of the well is marked by the granite pillars. The van nearest the camera appears to be the railway delivery van from Highgate Station.

153 *(overleaf)*. Highgate Hill, c.1885, by the Old Crown public house and tea-gardens. The cart is the Vestry's (later Council's) water-cart for laying the dust.

E A GARDENS
THE OLD
CROWN
SPIRIT

154. Hayhoe and Allen's Forge, North Road, c.1890. Mr. Hayhoe was the last blacksmith in Highgate. His forge is now Jackson's, the builder. Miss Hayhoe resided in Highgate until the Second World War.

155. Hornsey Lane, showing Turner's (later Spencer's) Farm — a popular resort for picnics, c.1875. The farm lands extended as far as what is now Northwood railway bridge.

156. The Woodman public house, decorated for Queen Victoria's Golden Jubilee in 1887. The VR is composed of coloured glass jars in which nightlights were inserted and lit by a taper each evening.

157. The Wellington public house, c.1880. The farmer (perhaps Mr. Lane of Manor Farm, where the golf course now is) has been on a rabbit shoot with his dog. There were still rabbits on the golf course fifty years later.

Archway

158. The Archway, 1885. The seven-foot railings replaced the original brick balustrade and stone parapet to prevent further suicides. The children attempting to climb the 'unclimbable' railings are most probably boys of St. Aloysius on their way home from school.

159. The toll-gate in 1873, showing the brickfields behind the toll-keeper and his lad. The tolls ceased in April 1876.

160 *(opposite, above).* The Archway Tavern in 1873, showing the beginning of Highgate Hill on the left of the picture.

161 *(opposite, below).* The Archway Tavern in 1888. Notice the changes since 1873 and the coming of the cable tramway in 1884. The Holborn Union Infirmary (now part of the Whittington Hospital) has risen behind the tavern, which has been 'modernised' into a typical Victorian public house. Notice, too, that litter is not a modern problem . . .

JOURNAL
ONE PENNY.
ENTIRE
WATNEY
ENTIRE

ARCHWAY TAVERN
PIMLICO ALES
NOTED STOUT STORES
WATNEY
WATNEY
WATNEY

162. A tram accident in the Archway Road, c.1906. There were several accidents caused by trams running away down Archway Road, and it was made compulsory for drivers to stop at the top of the hill and test their brakes before proceeding.

163. A bus accident in the Archway Road, c.1907. Note the cafe advertising 'A pot of tea for 2d.' and a three-course lunch for 1/-.